Tropical
Houses

The Deutsche Nationalbibliothek lists this publication in the Deutsche Nationalbibliographie; detailed bibliographical data are available on the internet at http://dnb.ddb.de

ISBN 978-3-03768-095-7
© 2012 by Braun Publishing AG
www.braun-publishing.ch

3rd edition 2013

Project coordination, layout: Michelle Galindo
Editorial staff: Judith Vonberg
Art direction: Michaela Prinz, Berlin

Michelle Galindo

Tropical Houses

Living in Paradise

BRAUN

Content

Preface

Don't we all share a dream of living a luxurious life in a tropical climate, far away from the stresses of everyday urban life? The houses featured in this volume offer to make that dream a reality. Embracing the vast surrounding expanses of sea, air, sky and vegetation, each project stands as a stunning complement to the natural world, which is celebrated, incorporated and reinvented in architectural forms, textures and colors. The reader is invited to imagine a life lived in perfect co-existence with nature where open-plan living spaces, sun-lit terraces, exotic gardens and tranquil pools beckon. Rough stone and timber find their way into interiors, while glass panels and wooden shutters open to welcome the external world. The architects whose work is represented here create spaces where the boundary between nature and architecture becomes indistinct, places where coconut trees and frangipanis, sand dunes and sea breezes can be enjoyed from the comfort of stunningly designed living spaces. From cozy, loft-style homes to palatial mansions, luxurious holiday retreats to functional family homes, this book brings together a collection of the most inspirational tropical houses for the reader's pure enjoyment. Renowned architects such as Bernades + Jacobsen Arquitetura, Wallflower Architecture + Design, and Guz Architects are represented alongside lesser known names, whose astounding creativity will surely propel them into spotlight.

In Singapore the lush tropical environment provides the inspiration for houses that bear a powerful visual connection with the natural world. Courtyards with pools and trees are established at the heart of the dwelling, which manifests itself as a masterpiece of synthesis – past and present, seclusion and openness, manmade and natural co-exist in perfect harmony. Natural ventilation, solar panels, on-site hydroelectric plants and energy efficient appliances are featured in a range of projects, many of which are self-sustainable, proving that luxury need not be compromised where environmental sensitivity is demanded. Indeed, many architects chose to use local materials and traditional building methods in the construction of creative masterpieces that stand as testaments to the power of architectural innovation. In Brazil, traditional building techniques and regional materials – clay and wood – are used to create a house where tradition and modernity, the primitive and the sophisticated mingle happily. Expansive terraces, a large swimming pool and breathtaking panoramic views at St. Barth generate an immediate sensation of peace and harmony that is echoed across projects from Costa Rica to Australia.

Tropical Houses features a stunning array of the most ambitious examples of tropical residential design from around the globe. Each project showcases how technology, planning and design can be applied sensitively to generate sustainable and luxurious homes in which living is pure pleasure.

from above to below, from left to right: infinity pool, terrace,
living room with floors covered in travertine

Peak House

St. Jean, Saint Barthélemy

Architect: Wolfgang Ludes +
Johannes Zingerle
Completion year: 2010
Materials: Dark brown wenge
wood from Africa (ceilings),
Italian travertine (floors)

Screened by a row of bamboo trees, the main building of Peak House is reached via an impressive stone stairway. Once past the trees, a stunning panoramic view of a white sandy beach and turquoise waters from the large terrace and pool area creates an atmosphere of peace and tranquility. The elements of earth, water and fire come together in this outdoor space with its pool, vegetation and outdoor fireplace, bridging the manmade and the natural. Complete privacy and breathtaking vistas can be enjoyed in all of the three buildings, each occupying a different level on the site's steep slope. A private terrace belonging to the master suite nestles into the cliff – an ideal spot to savor an exquisite sunset. This is a villa that exemplifies refined aesthetics and understated luxury.

from above to below, from left to right: bathroom with dark gray granite washbasin, covered terrace, living area, stairs leading to bedroom

from above to below: bedroom, dining room opens out to
terrace

12

from above to below, from left to right: pool area, resting area nestled into the cliff, private terrace with ocean views, terrace with breathtaking vistas

outdoor seating area

villa is set on a tropical paradise

Villa Dunes

Grande Salinas, Saint Barthélemy

Completion year: 2010
Materials: White oak parquet (floors), wenge

Overlooking the turquoise ocean to the south, and the steep tropical hills to the east, Villa Dunes offers a glorious location in which to forget the stress of urban life. Three floors of modern comfort and stylish living beckon, along with spacious wooden decks, heated pools, tropical gardens and elegant gray stonewalls. The deep brown wenge and white blasted oak wood of the contemporary furniture combine elegance with simplicity and ensure that the focus always remains on the rich and vibrant natural landscape that lies beyond the walls of this tropical house. However, with 1,490 square meters of exquisitely refined luxury and modern amenities, the lucky resident may be excused for choosing to enjoy that landscape only from the glorious comfort of the opulent master bedroom.

from above to below: living room, villa set on a steep tropical green and orange hills

from above to below: villa overlooks the turquoise ocean to
the south, lap pool

17

from above to below: living room extends out to terrace,
bedroom

from above to below: master bedroom with sweeping views, main entrance

living room with extended views onto landscape

panoramic view by night

Iseami House

Playa Carate, Peninsula de Osa, Costa Rica

Architect: Robles Arquitectos
Completion year: 2010
Materials: thermal-panels
(Versawall and Versapanel by
Centria) (walls), recycled plastic,
glass and steel (structure and
panels)

The Iseami House rests majestically on a hillside above the ocean on the hot and humid Peninsula de Osa in Costa Rica. A dazzling structure in white steel and glass, it represents both a contrast to and an integrated part of the natural surroundings. An on-site hybrid electricity system generates solar and hydroelectric energy, while ocean breezes and crosswinds naturally ventilate the open interior. Nearby mountains can be glimpsed through the skylights, which also control the sunlight entering the house, and expanses of glass allow unrestricted views of the vibrant tropical landscape and the sea below. This self-sustainable architectural jewel is the perfect location in which to savor the blue skies, ocean breezes and lush vegetation of Costa Rica.

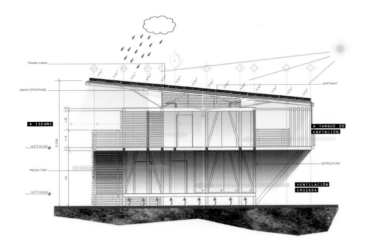

from above to below: diagrammatic section, kitchen with ocean
views

from above to below: terrace dining area, view from swimming pool to white steel and glass construction

23

from above to below, from left to right: living area, exterior
view by night, house rests on a hill above the ocean

from above to below: mountain view from kitchen, outdoor pool area, first floor plan

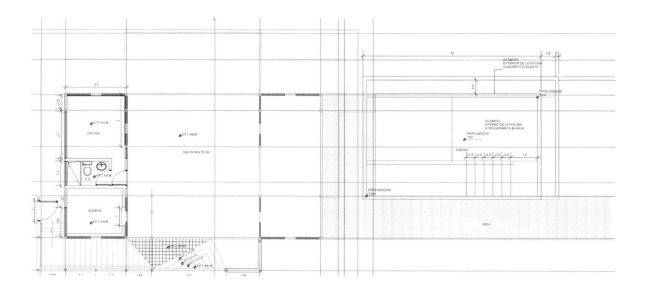

from above to below: house reflected in the pool, aerial view

from above to below: view to outdoor area from second floor,
master bedroom with opened retractable shutter panels

Torcida House

Osa Peninsula, Costa Rica

Architect: SPG Architects
Renewable Energy Systems:
Poderco S.A.
Completion year: 2009
Materials: steel, concrete, glass

Transformed from an abandoned steel and concrete structure into an elegant modern masterpiece, Torcida House is a breathtaking architectural triumph. Gleaming surfaces, glass expanses and white façades audaciously proclaim this structure as a visual anomaly amongst the dark tropical vegetation of Costa Rica. Yet environmental sensitivity was a priority and, as a result, natural cross breezes are exploited to provide ventilation and cabinetry was locally sourced from trees originally harvested from the site. Energy is generated by solar panels and an on-site hydroelectric plant, while interiors boast high-efficiency appliances and lighting, making this home wholly self-sustainable. Adjustable louvered and screened panels and a flexible building perimeter enable seamless interaction between the built environment and the natural setting. Technology, design and sensitivity coalesce to create a unique human environment in the heart of the tropics.

from above to below: floor plan, view of master bedroom from terrace

from above to below, from left to right: bathroom with teak shutterwalls, view
of driveway to the house, kitchen opens to the living / dining area

from above to below, from left to right: view of the pool and
living room from the terrace at dusk, kitchen, terrace

from above to below, from left to right: view of terraces and pool
by night, staircase, pool, floor plans

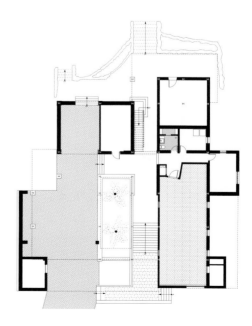

from left to right: outdoor rainshower, bedroom extends out to
the deck and a dipping pool

villa perched on a ridge

Pacuare Lodge

Turrialba, Costa Rica

Architect/designer: Roberto Fernandez and Daniel Peyer
Completion year: 2007
Materials: wood, palm thatch

The eco-friendly bungalows of Pacuare Lodge are surrounded by exuberant tropical foliage, nestled between the river and a private nature reserve. Inspired by its magnificent natural setting, these bungalows were designed and constructed to blend with the surrounding environment and have been officially recognized for being wholly sustainable and eco-friendly. The main building materials – wood and palm thatch – were locally sourced by Cabecar Indians and each bungalow uses solar-heated water and low-impact septic systems and operates without electricity. Locally crafted wood furnishings, hand-hewn timber beams, wrought iron chandeliers and tropical flowers create an inviting ambience of rustic splendor. Combining simple luxury and unity with nature in its purest and most primitive state, Pacuare Lodge sets a new standard in Costa Rican living.

from above to below, from left to right: indoor/outdoor rainshower, interior view to ceiling made of palm leaves, covered terrace, outdoor shower surrounded by a stonewall

from above to below: hammock with rainforest view, bedroom

from above to below, from left to right: free-standing bathtub with open views to rainforest, views of the Pacuare River from deck, interior with natural design

from above to below, from left to right: dining area, bridge leading to villa, view to villa from garden

from left to right: house set on a tropical garden, wind cools down the interior

wooden house on top of the concrete house

Casa Tropical

Mundaú-Ceará, Brazil

Architect: Camarim Architects
Project Architects: Vasco Correia & Patricia Sousa
Completion year: 2008
Materials: wood, glass panels

Located in a fishing village in northern Brazil, this holiday retreat is a stunning complement to the natural elements that surround it. The architects rejected a conventional compact volume in favor of a more permeable structure. An open gallery enveloped in a wooden skin surrounds all three floors, sheltering the interior from the intense tropical sun, while allowing a cool mountain breeze to waft through it. Like the open roof, the gallery is a space where the boundary between nature and architecture becomes indistinct, a place where coconut trees and earth, dunes and sea can be contemplated and enjoyed. Energy and drinking water are gathered from natural sources – sun, wind and rain – further strengthening the close bond between Casa Tropical and its lush, natural surroundings.

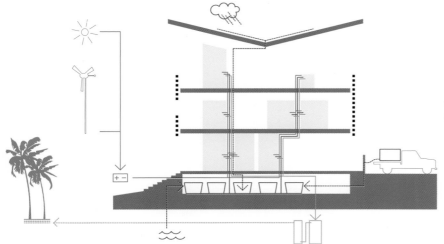

from above to below: weather diagram, view to wide gallery for circulation on the outside of the building

from above to below, from left to right: detail gallery, dining area with extended views to landscape,
wooden roof and walls of the gallery shelter the building from the sun

from above to below, from left to right: contemporary interior, interior
with panoramic views to tropical site, mosquito net covering bed

from above to below: suspended wooden roof, bathroom, floor plans

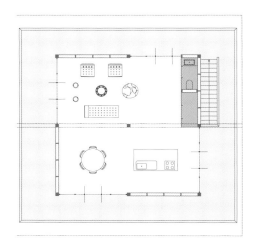

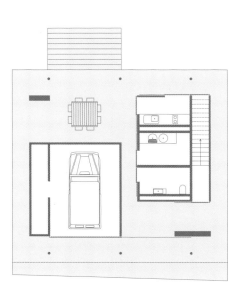

from above to below, from left to right: interior/exterior, wooden
deck extends to surrounding landscape, floating Cumaru stairway,
narrow bridge crosses over the center of the living room

kitchen/dining area extends out to the surrounding flora

House in Iporonga

Iporonga, Brazil

Architect: Arthur Casas Studio
Completion year: 2008
Materials: Cumaru wood
(floors), glass

In designing his own home, Arthur Casas has manifested the ultimate expression of his relationship to the surrounding world. House in Iporonga is positioned deep within the Brazilian forest — the defining Brazilian landscape, according to Casas. Two symmetrical rectangular cubes face each other on the north and south sides of the site, connected by two retractable 11-meter high glass walls. The entire exterior is paneled in Cumaru wood that blends effortlessly into the surrounding forest. Cumaru is also used inside as flooring where it stands out boldly against the stark white walls — the only "color" found in the minimalist space. Outside, an infinity pool appears to be spilling over to soak the surrounding flora in a visual display of unity with the natural context. Casas has perfectly accomplished the creation of a personal retreat, a space in which to relax, recharge and daydream.

from above to below, from left to right: exterior view, living room with open views to surrounding, wooden terrace

from above to below: outdoor dining table, terrace steps down to tropical garden, ground floor plan

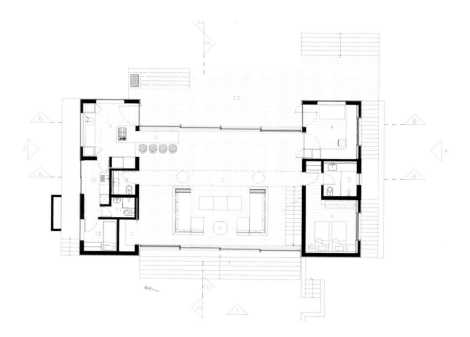

relaxation/bar area

cantilevered front volume

FP House

Pampulha, Belo Horizonte, Brazil

Architect: João Diniz Arquitetura
Landscape design: Mercado Verde / Firmino Fiuza
Structural engineers (concrete structure): Marcello Cláudio and Sigefredo Fiuza
Completion year: 2010
Materials: concrete (walls), wood (floors), bamboo (roof)

Built on the margins of the Pampulha lagoon in Belo Horizonte, a site bursting with architectural significance, the FP House makes its own compelling architectural statement. The house, with its sequence of ascending and descending steps and levels, works in harmony with the sloping site, establishing a fascinating dialogue of complementarily between the structure and its context.

A route from the street leads directly to the roof, where the observer is confronted with a spectacular vista. Clean lines and simple white façades combine to create this striking visual landmark. It stands as a testament to the power of architectural innovation.

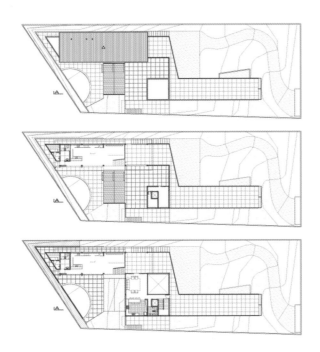

from above to below, from left to right: floor plans, general
view, steps to terrace

from above to below, from left to right: interior spaces housed underneath slanted wooden roof, bedroom, elongated terrace

from above to below: indoor/outdoor area with slanted roof, areal view of living room, three-dimensional drawing

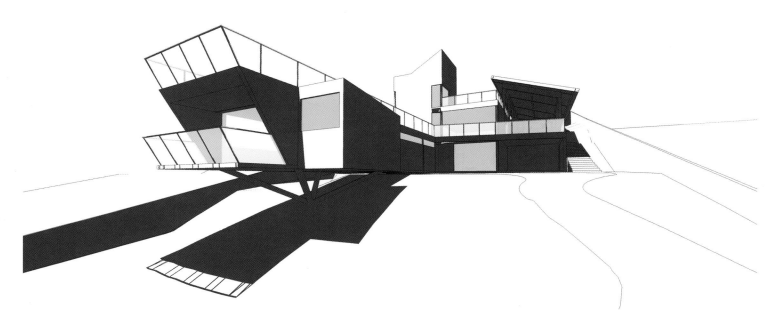

Indoor-outdoor spaces

façade opens onto gardens

GR House

São Paulo, Brazil

Architect: Bernardes + Jacobsen Arquitetura
Lighting design: iluz – Studio de Iluminação
Structural engineer: Leão e Associados
Landscape design: Gil Fialho Planejamento e Paisagismo Tropical
Completion year: 2008
Materials: glass, white marble (floors), timber wood (floors and façades)

The GR House offers an oasis of calm in the midst of a populous urban setting. Although situated on a narrow plot between two homes, a sense of seclusion and serenity is generated by the abundant vegetation around the dwelling. Wide openings, minimal visible support and catwalks with minimal walling promote circulation and openness between interior and exterior, house and world.

A multitude of openings and extensive use of glass allow natural light to flood the highly stylish internal spaces. Glass is complemented by white marble and timber, a pairing of the luxurious and the unrefined that defines the GR House, enabling it to blend seamlessly with its surroundings.

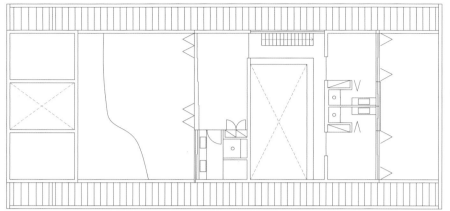

from above to below: first floor plan, detail of façade by night

from above to below: closed façade, living room extends out
to garden

from above to below: wooden stairs, exterior night view from garden

from above to below: second floor with open views to garden,
section

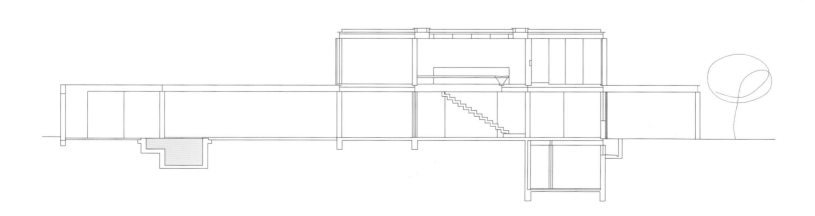

second volume built with pre-fabricated wood structure

view to open interior with "muxarabi" windows filtering light

Pier House

Paraty, Rio de Janeiro, Brazil

Architect: Gabriel Grinspum + Mariana Simas
Completion year: 2009
Materials: whitewashed façades, "muxarabi", metal tile and wood

The Pier House represents the architectural embodiment of the noble savage. Located in a tropical fjord accessible only by boat, the site itself is reminiscent of a lost paradise. Drawing on ancient regional construction methods and local materials, and acknowledging the need to preserve the dense surrounding vegetation, the architects created a sustainable, environmentally friendly cottage-like home that houses a boat during the week and its owners at the weekend. Whitewashed façades, "muxarabi", metal tile and wood mingle in a heady explosion of sophistication and simplicity. Sliding walls, wide-open windows and permeable façades allow natural lighting and ventilation. Like the boat it shelters, the Pier House symbolizes humanity and nature co-existing peacefully. In this space, worldly cares can be forgotten and the human spirit is granted the freedom to dream.

from above to below, from left to right: detail of "muxarabi" window screens, house slopes down the hill, view towards house from tropical fjord

from above to below: house set on dense vegetation of rainforest, section

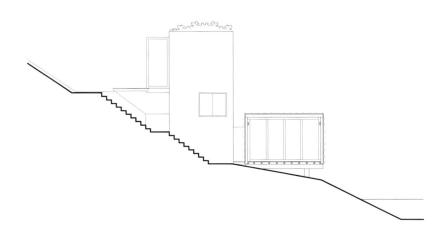

façade detail

sliding latticed wooden panels open up the interior

Bahia House

Salvador, Brazil

Architect: studio mk27 –
Marcio Kogan + Suzana
Glogowski + Samanta Cafardo
Interior design: Diana
Radomysler
Landscape design: Renata Tilli
Completion year: 2010
Materials: clay (roof), wood
(ceiling), sliding latticed wooden
panels (exterior walls), stone
(walls)

Inspired by rich Brazilian building traditions and traditional local materials, the architects of Bahia House used wood and clay and natural ventilation methods to create a structure that exists in harmony with both its present surroundings and the centuries of history that have formed modern Brazil. It is organized simply around a central patio to maximize natural ventilation, which is further encouraged by the sliding latticed wooden panels that form the exterior walls, inspired by Arabian and Portuguese architectural influences. Wooden ceilings and clay roofs designed in consciously rustic style pay homage to a traditional, more natural way of life. This house proves that the past need not be eradicated by, but can instead be incorporated into contemporary architecture. History, tradition and culture are resurrected and reinvented in a home that celebrates what it means to be Brazilian.

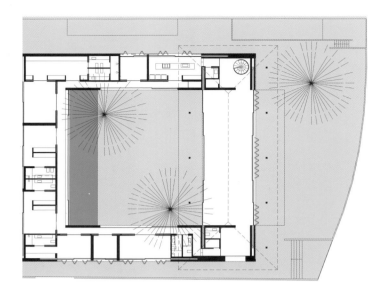

from above to below, from left to right: ground floor plan, wooden ceiling, kitchen, bedroom opens out to garden

from above to below: dining room, side view of closed façade

from above to below, from left to right: interior with open floor plan, detail of clay roof, view to grassed garden and mango trees

from above to below: extended deck, garden, section

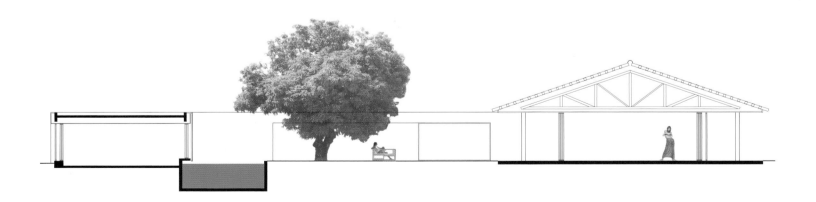

69

from left to right: living room, dining room

wooden panels can open and close

JH House

São Paulo, Brazil

Architect: Bernardes + Jacobsen Arquitetura
Lighting design: Godoy & Associados
Structural engineer: Leão e Associados
Landscape design: Isabel Duprat Paisagismo
Vertical garden design: Gica Mesiara – Quadro Vivo
Completion year: 2008

Inspired by the world's most luxurious five-star resorts, JH House, a modern home in São Paulo, is a hidden oasis. Quietly concealed behind a green grass wall, this extravagant dwelling boasts stone and wood for its exterior, with a spectacular outdoor living area at its heart. Palm trees reach high above the pool, which stands between the stunning poolside lounge and the glass-enclosed

modern interior. Overhead, wooden panels can be opened to reveal the blue skies above. These functional shades are also a superb feature of the interior, allowing for bright, naturally lit spaces and blurring the conventional boundary between indoor and outdoor. A minimalist white palette and simple but luxurious details combine to create internal spaces that invite total relaxation.

71

from above to below, from left to right: outdoor living area with lap pool, front wooden façade with green grass wall, interior

from above to below: detail of glazed façade, sections

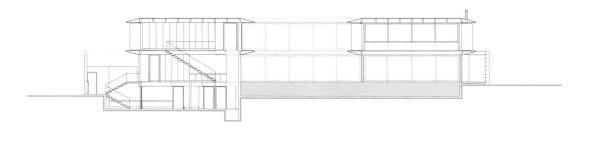

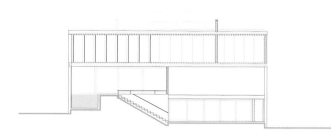

from above to below: terrace with outdoor living and overhanging roof, interior with panoramic view to seafront

from above to below: interior with open views to surroundings, exterior envelope

La Isla Beach House

Playa La Isla, Asia, Cañete, Peru

Architect: Juan Carlos Doblado
Structural engineer: Pedro Moscoso
Completion year: 2008
Materials: concrete, glass

Located opposite the sea, overlooking nearby islands in the South Pacific, La Isla Beach House establishes a relationship between man and nature, desert and sea. It offers both a private space in which humans can relax in the midst of harsh desert surroundings, and also an open invitation to enjoy the stunning ocean view. A solid geometric volume was constructed and then drilled, gen-erating an intimate and hidden sunken courtyard. Through this, and through the cantilevered roof of the front terrace, a vertical relationship with the sky is developed that complements the horizontal dialogue with the sea. Opacity and transparency, privacy and exteriority exist in a comple-mentary dialectic, enabling the resident to feel wholly at home whilst engaging with the surrounding world.

from above to below, from left to right: sunken courtyard, dining/living room, kitchen

from above to below: plunge pool and view to rear façade, section

from above to below, from left to right: main entrance, planted interior, jacuzzi

from above to below, from left to right: master bathroom, bedroom with panoramic view, planted interior with wooden stepping surface

Cabo House

Buenos Aires, Argentina

Architect: Andres Remy Arquitectos
Completion year: 2008
Materials: concrete, glass

The clients expressed a desire for a cozy, compact and functional home: Cabo House is the supreme embodiment of all these wishes. Opening towards the back, the house takes full advantage of the northern sun and spectacular views of the lake adjoining the property on two sides. At the front south side, the residents' privacy is fully and respectfully preserved. A central two-story space, filled with vegetation, invites free air circulation and welcomes natural light into the interior spaces, transforming a compact volume into a grand meeting place of the architectural and the natural. Located on the edge of the site, the circular pool counteracts the building's straight lines and blends visually with the lake beyond, a serene reminder of the natural world to which this project pays homage.

from above to below, from left to right: front façade, kitchen,
view to planted interior from second floor

from above to below, from left to right: sliding glass doors, green interior, view of interior from garden, floor plans

from left to right: jacuzzi with open views, view from swimming pool towards garden

interior view from garden

Devoto House

Buenos Aires, Argentina

Architect: Andres Remy
Arquitectos
Completion year: 2008
Materials: stone (walls),
concrete, glass

Working on a tight urban site between two existing buildings, the architects of Devoto House have created a spacious, tropical retreat that boldly contravenes the conventions of a standard urban home. Using all their ingenuity, they established a 500 square meter house on a site of 18 by 24 meters. To ensure the building did not overwhelm the outdoor elements – a lush garden and elevated pool – the second story has a smaller floor

plan than the stories below. The grassed area, a tranquil natural space in a busy urban setting, leads the way to the entrance of the house. The natural element penetrates the interior with an extensive stonewall, softening the hard angles and white expanses that dominate the internal spaces. Natural and architectural simplicity join forces to generate a functional, yet spectacular, family home.

from above to below, from left to right: living area, dining/living, staircase

from above to below, from left to right: swimming pool is elevated from the ground, detail swimming pool, living room, ground floor plan

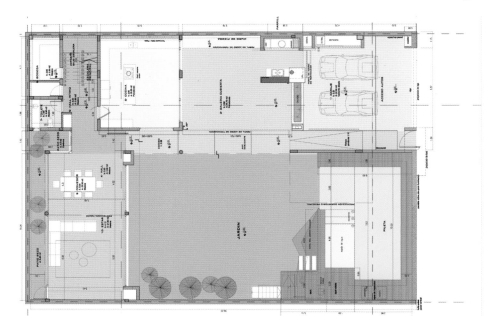

house/loft set on the cliff-face

loft-like living interior opens out to the wilderness

Singita Lebombo

Kruger National Park, South Africa

Architect: OMM Design Workshop/ Andrew Makin and Janina Masojada
Interior design: Cécile & Boyd's
Structural engineers: Arup
Completion year: 2008 (refurbished)
Materials: glass, steel, local timber wood, thatch, earth walls and screed floors

Singita Lebombo offers rare solitude and the ultimate in luxury on prime game viewing land recognized globally for its diversity and formidable concentration of big game and frequent leopard sightings. The loft-like lodges are infused with the glamour and elegance of Singita, feature contemporary finishes and sumptuous furnishings. From the sweeping wooden decks, the observer can enjoy the theatre unfolding across the vast plains, while the lap pool beckons invitingly – a refreshing dip in the heat of the day. The resident can enjoy dinner in the boma before spending the evening sleeping under the stars on the elegant private terrace. Like the Lebombo Euphorbia tree after which it was named, the design of Lebombo Lodge is one of a kind, a glorious architectural anomaly in wild surroundings.

from above to below: loungers by lap pool, double-height living area with open views

from above to below: lap pool at dusk, view of the Nwanetsi river from elevated deck

indoor-outdoor living spaces

exterior view from swimming pool area

Marcus Beach House

Queensland, Australia

Architect: Bark Design Architects
Builder: Wall's Quality Homes
Structural Engineer: Meecham Engineers
Completion year: 2009
Materials: timber wood (structure), polycarbonate (staircase), glass

The natural, coastal setting of the Marcus Beach House provided the perfect inspiration for this unique dwelling. Drawing on the rudimentary yet arresting style of the beach houses and fishing shacks that line the Queensland coast, the design pays homage to a defining feature of the state's cultural heritage, whilst manifesting the glorious possibilities of contemporary architecture. The occupant dwells in a world of transparency and dynamic patterns of light and shadow through which natural breezes roam, dispersing the boundary between indoor and outdoor, man-made and natural space. When viewed from the street, the garage is almost hidden, allowing the dwelling to blend with its surroundings, both coastal and architectural. This is a building in an intimate relationship with the world around it.

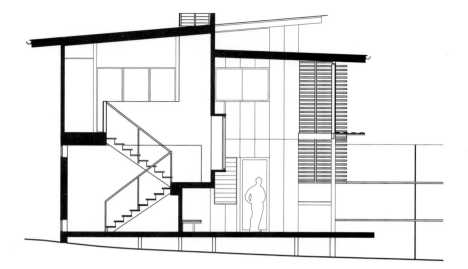

from above to below: section, dining area on extended, covered deck

from above to below: view from corridor towards garden, lay-
ers of transparency integrating indoor-outdoor spaces

from above to below: rear view, front façade

from above to below, from left to right: outdoor bench, library, staircase, elevation

from left to right: living room with ocean view, entry covered pathway

swimming pool / courtyard

Albatross Avenue House

Gold Coast, Queensland, Australia

Architect: BGD Architects
Interior design: Sonia Hill and Edge Design + Interiors
Lighting design: Tony Dowthwaite
Landscape design: Imagine IDG
Completion year: 2008
Materials: timber wood, stone and glass

Albatross Avenue House takes full advantage of its superb waterfront location. Twenty-five meters of glazing on the ground floor allow unrestricted indulgence in the ocean view, which can also be enjoyed from the bedrooms on the upper level. A private yet expansive pool and entertaining core confirm this residence as an oasis that offers luxurious, aesthetically interesting, adaptable internal spaces. The interior is dominated by warm textures, sandstone, timber and glazing, which combine to create a tropical, modern and cozy ambience. Amenities are centralized enabling easy access and the house is ventilated by natural breezes, controlled by louvred glazing. Mature trees and palms frame the house and swimming pool, natural features that complement and soften the polished concrete and rough stone finishes. Lit at night, this landscape of water, timber battens and a palm frond becomes a dramatic arena, the perfect stage for a tale of man finding contentment in co-existence with nature.

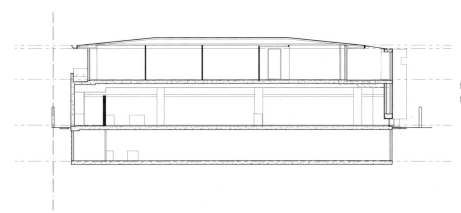

from above to below, from left to right: section, entry path, beach-front elevation

from above to below, from left to right: interior view from terrace, lounge, interior courtyard with swimming pool

from above to below: open floor plan interior, fireplace

from above to below: terrace, section

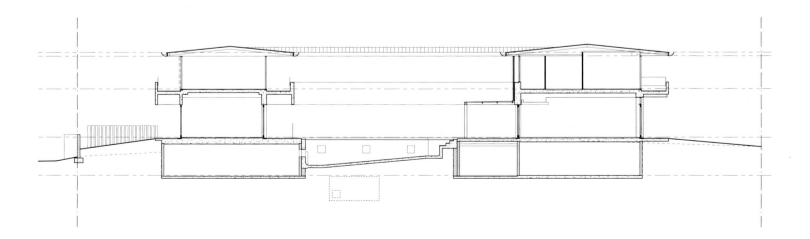

from above to below, from left to right: ocean view, reflective pool,
view across to dining room from living room

entry pathway divides living volumes

Ala Moana

Hamilton Island, Whitsundays, Queensland, Australia

Architect: Omiros One Architecture
Decorator: Chris Elliot
Completion year: 2009
Materials: rosewood, stone, glass, zinc (roof)

Taking its name from a Hawaiian phrase meaning "ocean pathways", Ala Moana is a stunning architectural gem boasting uninhibited ocean views and combining luxury, tranquility and privacy. A journey of discovery along a meandering path awaits the visitor to this house, who is introduced to its various aspects, textures and features while still at a distance. Once inside, the glorious view rightfully takes center stage, framed by a series of architectural shapes that work hand in hand with the surroundings to enhance the experience. The internal reflective pool rolls through the site to the open view at the front, fusing with the sky and appearing to spill into the ocean beyond. Minimal visual impact was achieved by breaking down the mass into smaller articulated parts, each set at different levels and following the natural slope. The result is lightness and transparency combined with grandeur, environmental sensitivity with opulence.

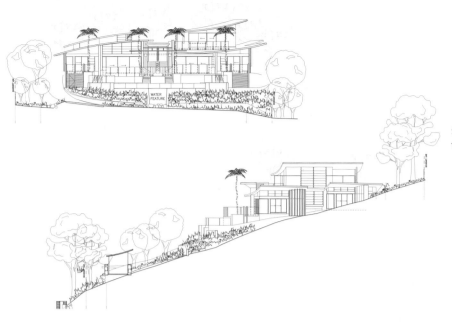

from above to below, from left to right: elevations, exterior night view, bathtub, main entrance

from above to below: bedroom with breathtaking views, view to dining room from living room volume

105

outdoor dining by swimming pool

infinity pools blends with ocean

Cliff House

Chowara, Kerala, India

Architect: Khosla Associates
Structural engineer: Manjunath & Co.
Landscape design: Hariyalee Consultants
Completion year: 2010
Materials: timber, rough slate, natural local kota stone (floors), glass, concrete and polished cement

True to their initial desire to create a house that embraces the vast surrounding expanses of sea, air and sky, Khosla Associates kept much of the built area open and intelligently permeable to the elements. Natural light and breezes are welcomed into the interior through slatted wooden shutters, a simple solution to the hot climate. Ample overhangs also provide protection from the fierce sun and monsoon rains, while still allowing the natural and built spaces to mingle. A highlight of Cliff House is the striking asymmetrical sloping roof set against the fronds of a coconut plantation. The canopy roof is clad on the underside with eco-friendly timber that offsets with warmth the large expanses of kota flooring, concrete and polished cement. Not only is this house a sophisticated living space, but also it invites participation in the world beyond, an Indian coastal community co-existing perfectly with nature.

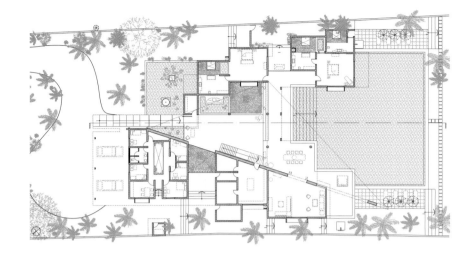

from above to below, from left to right: ground floor plan, canopy roof, open-enclosed living area, view towards bathroom

from above to below: bedroom with sliding, louvered wooden
walls, open bathroom

from above to below, from left to right: exterior view from
swimming pool, dining table with open ocean view, pond

from above to below: window detail, staircase, section

from above to below, from left to right: house set inside a functioning coconut plantation, view of one of the wooden houses from courtyard, interior

from above to below, from left to right: courtyard, 7.6 meter pool, wooden louvers open living areas onto the courtyard

Palmyra House

Nandgaon, Maharashtra, India

Architect: Studio Mumbai Architects
Completion year: 2008
Materials: Palmyra palm wood

This two-story timber house, built as a weekend retreat, lies in the shade of an extensive coconut grove on agricultural land facing the sea. The functions of the house are placed within two oblong masses slightly offset from one another, whose façades are characterized by louvers made from the trunks of the local Palmyra palm. Ain wood, local basalt and sand from the site were all incorpo-rated into the structure, which thus pays homage to the surrounding world of which it has become a part. The louvers on the elevations and shade provided by the coconut trees enable passive cooling and water is harvested from three on-site wells. The result of these measures is a quietly compelling, unassuming and inspirational project that is fully integrated into its landscape.

airy and open interiors

from above to below: view by night, floor plans

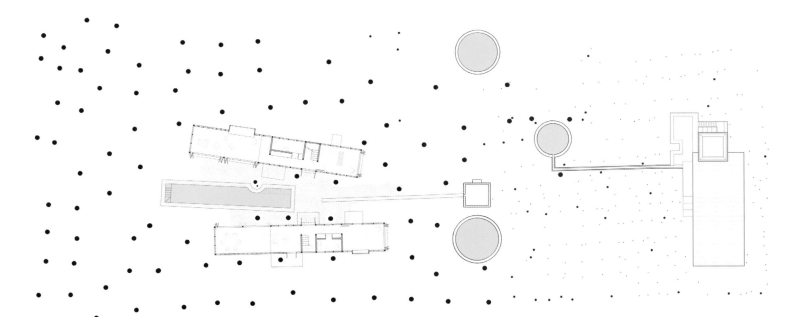

from above to below: planted courtyard, view across rice field,
villas set on a lush green of Balinese rice terraces

oceanview from infinity pool

Alila Villas Soori

Bali, Indonesia

Architect: SCDA Architects
Completion year: 2011
Materials: gray and black volcanic stone and polished teak, glass

Alila Villas Soori has brought new meaning to stylish, luxurious and yet relaxed beachfront living. All the villas in this magnificent property were sensitively designed to maximize views of the surrounding beach, sea and paddy fields, while still maintaining a sense of privacy and shelter. Each villa is designed with elegant interconnected spaces that blend seamlessly together to create a harmonious flow from the interior to exterior space. Large expanses of glass and sliding doors provide easy enjoyment of and access to pool areas and the sea beyond. Sunlit days can be spent on the terrace, in the pool, or relaxing in the luxurious indoor living areas, while evenings offer stunning sunsets, complemented by the villas themselves, which are subtly and stylishly lit. A place to unwind and rediscover harmony with oneself and the world.

from above to below, from left to right: master bathroom, infinity pool around the villa, outdoor lounge area, ocean view from main villa

from above to below: exterior view, outdoor living area

from above to below: pool area, terrace steps down to infinity
pool and garden

from above to below, from left to right: bathtub with view to infinity pool, bedroom, villa entrance, window detail

from above to below: private garden, living modules detail

living area features an open-plan design

Alila Uluwatu

Bali, Indonesia

Architects: WOHA
Completion year: 2011
Materials: lava rock (roof),
bamboo (ceiling)

This cluster of buildings, terraces, pools and gardens located on a limestone cliff on Bali's Bukit Peninsula was inspired by Bukit's dramatic, savannah landscape. Accordingly, the Alila Villas Uluwatu achieves a harmony with nature palpable to all who spend time there. Using sustainable wood for construction and working with the dry savannah vegetation and gently sloping site, not against them, contributed towards the achievement of Green Globe certification, the highest level of Environmentally

Sustainable Design. The flat roofs are laid with batu chandi, a local porous Javanese rock that provides insulation and water absorption to support plant life, and blends in with the local landscape. As well as being aesthetically pleasing, the jigsaw-like exteriors of the pavilion are made from a mixture of recycled wood and bronze, allowing breezes to circulate while maintaining privacy.

123

from above to below, from left to right: view from pool area, hillside villa, aerial view towards swimming pool, view across from swimming pool of other villas

from above to below: main villa pavilion, open-enclosed living area

from above to below: bedroom, indoor/outdoor living spaces

from above to below, from left to right: master bathroom, bathroom opens out to private garden, façade detail, private pool

from above to below: house overhangs into the garden, garden view

view from swimming pool towards the different houses

Wilkinson Road

Singapore, Singapore

Architect: K2LD Architects
Completion year: 2011
Materials: glass (wall panels),
timber (façades), granite stone
(walls), handmade panels plant
fibers (internal screens and
ceiling panels)

Arranged around a central garden and sharing fishponds
and a swimming pool, these three houses exist both as in-
dependent dwellings and as complementary, communica-
tive structures. Not only does each house exist in dialogue
with its neighbors, but also glass panels in the lower
volumes enable living and dining areas to be opened to
the external world, establishing communication between
interior and exterior spaces. Within the houses, granite
and handmade panels of plant fibers bring a sense of the

natural into the manmade dwellings. Wrapped around the
upper volumes, timber screen panels act as a protective
second skin and offer shading and privacy. The inhabitants of these houses cannot fail to forget the hustle and
bustle of urban life outside the gates, replaced in this
small patch of land by a sense of harmony engendered
by the intelligent integration of the built with the natural
environment.

from above to below, from left to right: interior view, planted private garden, timber screen panels wrapped around the upper volumes, covered terrace

from above to below: living area, exterior view

from above to below: living area opens out to fish pond,
dining room with glass panels

from above to below: detail of timber screen panels, dining room
opens out to the garden, covered terrace

from above to below: rooftop plants help to cool down the house, indoor-outdoor bathtub

from above to below: detail entrance, nature is integrated seamlessly into the interiors

Cluny House

Singapore, Singapore

Architect: Guz Architects
Completion year: 2009
Materials: glass, wood, stone

Cluny House embodies a unique and highly elegant combination of a modern glass structure and lush greenery. A roof bursting with foliage and flat green lawns both evoke and echo the fertile tropical environment. Forming a focal point, the pool cools the airflow and reflects the dappled sunlight and surrounding trees, creating an atmosphere of calming tranquility. Structured around the central pool, the interior spaces are reminiscent of outdoor cabanas, simple and open to engagement with nature. This comfortable, luxurious and sustainable family home showcases technology and design applied sensitively in the creation of an understated palace of serenity.

from above to below: courtyard filled with a thousand plants,
detail inside swimming pool

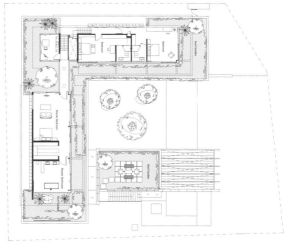

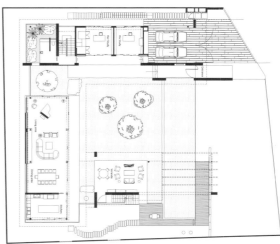

from left to right, from above to below: open dining area, floor plans, section

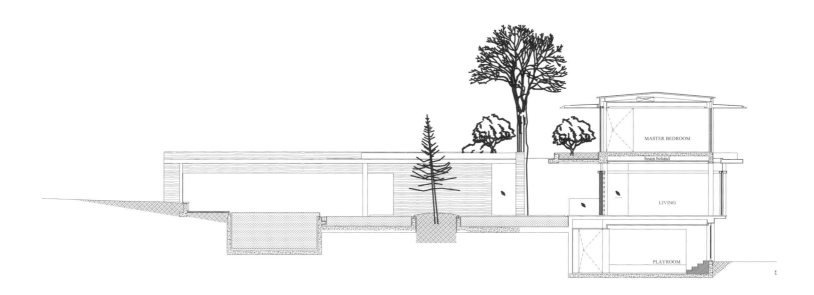

from left to right: dark reflecting pond surrounds the pavilion, circular void connects the entrance foyer to the pavilion above

exterior view

Water-Cooled House

Bukit Timah, Singapore

Architect: Wallflower
Architecture + Design
Completion year: 2009
Materials: concrete, glass,
wood, stone

Tucked away from the road and bordered by a verdant screen of mature trees, the house was inspired by its lush tropical surroundings. It exudes coolness and tranquility, a result of the constant presence of flowing, calm and bubbling water and the warm breezes that blow across the site. To allow the occupant to fully benefit from the splendor of the diverse natural environment, the main living room and study were located in a pavilion on the second story, from which the eye can wander unobstructed across

the fertile landscape. Enclosing and supporting structures were kept to a minimum so that this elevated vista might achieve its full potential. A minimal spiral staircase, touching down within the entrance foyer, guides visitors up to this pavilion where the natural world can be enjoyed from the comfort of a stunningly designed living space.

from above to below, from left to right: pond surrounding
pavilion, side view, entrance foyer

from above to below: entrance detail, pavilion in second floor, section

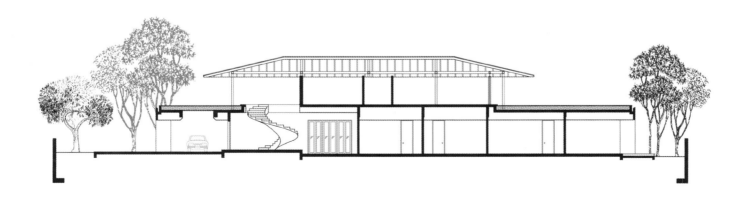

from above to below, from left to right: wooden floating roof, curved staircase, pathway along the pond leads to the bedrooms, koi pond in ground floor

from above to below: light filters into bathroom,
ground floor plan

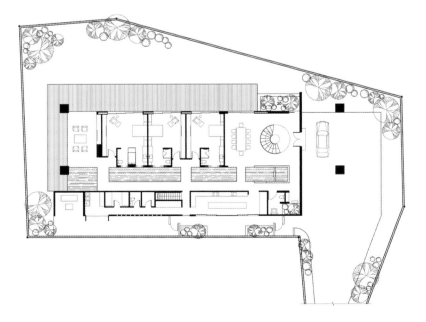

from above to below: view from swimming pool, kitchen

from left to right: façade detail, view into interior spaces through glazed façade

Binjai Park

Singapore, Singapore

Architect: K2LD Architects
Completion year: 2011
Materials: aluminum (walls), glass (wall panels), timber (screens)

The highly striking modern façade of this house at Binjai Park expresses the architectural concept behind it legibly and with finesse. The main volume reads as aluminum clad bracket, its thin edge folding around to enclose the glass structure. Juxtaposed against the flat metallic cladding, randomly placed timber screens over the secondary volume provide protection both from prying eyes and from the afternoon sun. A tranquil pool runs the entire length of the site and, along with the garden, forms a continuous backdrop to the internal living areas. As a result, interior and exterior spaces merge into each other – natural and architectural elements transgress their conventional boundaries. The undiluted form of the building and the simplicity of the materials demonstrate a daring and ultimately successful approach to sophisticated modern tropical living.

from above to below: exterior view, rear façade

from above to below, from left to right: aluminum clad bracket and glass structure volume, structural detail, living encased in glass with view towards swimming pool

from above to below: bedroom, living room with glass sliding
doors

from above to below: central staircase, view by night

from left to right: living room opens on both sides to swimming pool and to second courtyard, hardwood louvers

internal garden with swimming pool

Enclosed Open House

East Coast, Singapore

Architect: Wallflower
Architecture + Design
Completion year: 2009
Materials: wood (louvers),
glass, granite (courtyard)

The transparent volumes of the Enclosed Open House allow a continuous view from the entrance foyer and pool, through the formal living area to the internal garden court-yard and formal dining area in the second volume. This extraordinary sense of openness is complemented by a well-conceived layout that internalizes spaces such as the pool and garden in order to maintain privacy. The house

is passively cooled by breezes that move unobstructed between the courtyards and through the living, dining and pool house interiors. Adjustable solid hardwood louvers in the second story allow breezes and sunlight to filter into the upper level. Unencumbered space, dappled sunlight and the hush of water rippling on a pond combine to create a priceless atmosphere of serenity.

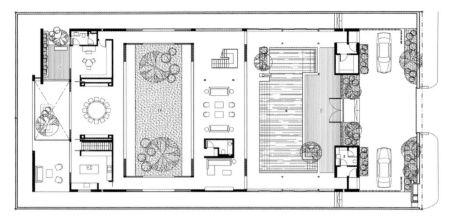

from above to below, from left to right: first floor plan, main entrance, covered exterior pathway, central staircase with glass panels

from above to below: transparency at ground level between courtyards, free-standing bathtub in master bathroom

from above to below: view to main entrance from driveway,
view across courtyard to living room from dining room

from above to below: hardwood louvers cover front façade,
section

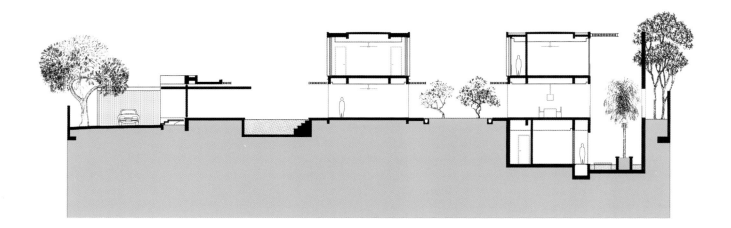

from above to below: curved roof symbolizing the sea waves,
interior with sea views

swimming pool linking the house with the landscape

Fish House

Singapore, Singapore

Architect: Guz Architects
Engineers: C&S Engineers and
Herizal Fitri Consultants
Completion year: 2009

This spectacular modern tropical bungalow seamlessly combines comfort and engagement with nature. Open, breezy interiors enable natural ventilation to counteract the hot and humid climate. From every room, residents enjoy breathtaking, uninhibited views, their eye led first to the clear blue pool in the garden, and then, beyond that, to the unbounded, restless ocean. This powerful visual connection with the vast natural world evolves further in both the curved roof, evoking the ocean's eternally rolling waves, and the lush green roof, a space designed, it would seem, to inspire dreams. This harmonious visual relationship with nature is complemented by solar panels, which generate sustainable, environmentally friendly energy to the whole house.

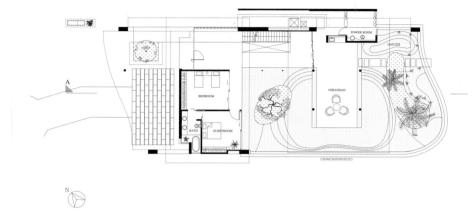

from above to below: first floor plan, master bathroom

from above to below: exterior view from garden, swimming pool around the house

from above to below: exterior view by night, entertainment room below ground level

from above to below: detail of curved green roof, view of swimming pool from covered pathway, section

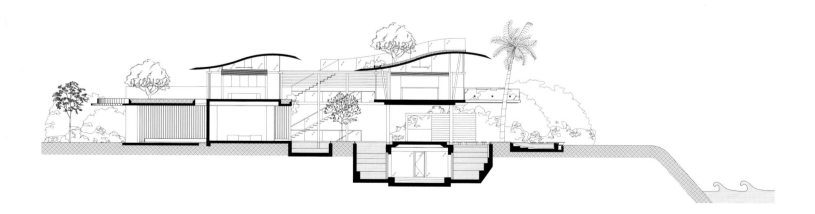

from above to below, from left to right: inner planted courtyard, swimming pool, staircase leading to swimming pool

rear façade by night

72 Sentosa Cove

Singapore, Singapore

Architect: ONG&ONG
Architects
Completion year: 2009
Materials: teak wood, glass, concrete

This is a home that can endure the tropics with minimal environmental impact by making use of available resources. Four levels of social and private spaces make up the building. To maintain privacy, internal spaces face inward towards a multifunctional courtyard which acts as circulation pivot and light well, while also serving as a striking visual focal point. Dense, verdant foliage also provides a natural means for additional privacy. The building's slimmer east and west façades contrast the broader façades to the north and south, effectively regulating natural lighting and ventilation. A stunning pitched roof, with a series of repeating slopes, allows for additional skylight openings. This is a house that achieves great sophistication with just a few masterful strokes.

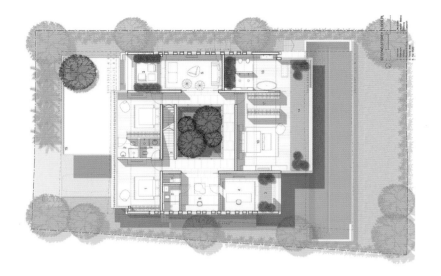

from above to below, from left to right: second floor plan, dining/kitchen, living room

from above to below, from left to right: green wall by driveway, bathroom sinks, free-standing bathtub opens out to surroundings

from above to below, from left to right: rear glazed façade,
view to living room from courtyard by night, boundary garden

from above to below, from left to right: bedroom, central staircase, hallway, first floor plan

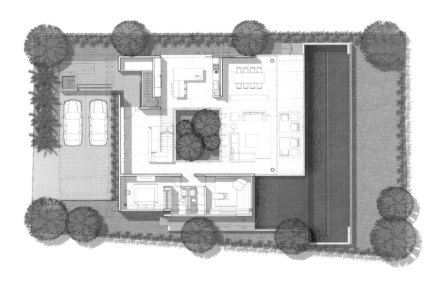

from above to below, from left to right: open and airy living room, covered outdoor living room, interior with Sri Lankan decoration

house is set in tropical gardens

River House

Balapitiya, Sri Lanka

Designer: Taru
Completion year: 2011 (refurbishment)
Materials: wood, stone and polished cement

Set amid a wide expanse of verdant land on a belt of coconut plantations, the secluded retreat of River House is a sanctuary for the body and the spirit — an idyllic hideaway that offers style, comfort and absolute serenity. Traditional craftsmanship using wood, stone and polished cement combines with Taru's own colorful and symmetrical style, seamlessly blending antique splendor and contemporary comfort. A profusion of Asian antiques throughout the interior celebrates the region's cultural heritage and generates a sense of the exotic. Sri Lankan chic, clean modern lines and primitive tradition mingle gloriously in both the interior and the exterior architecture. Inhabitants are invited to relax in the Jacuzzi, take a dip in the glistening pool, or even travel up river, reach for the fishing rod and reside for a while with nature.

from above to below: exterior view, slate plunge pool

from above to below, from left to right: bathroom, bedroom
with vaulted ceilings, foyer, outdoor dining area, pond

from above to below, from left to right: exterior view from driveway, bathtub, veranda with antique chaise loungers

from left to right: central two-storied courtyard, veranda

Kandy House

Kandy, Sri Lanka

Architect: MICD Associates/ Channa Daswatte
Completion year: 2011 (refurbishment)
Materials: wood, stone and polished cement

In the restoration of a 200-year-old palatial villa, the architects were commissioned to retain the charisma of the original while creating a luxury dwelling befitting the 21st century. The tranquil and seductive setting of the Kandy House offers beautiful landscaped gardens around the master house with a pool at the foot of the valley garden. The main house is designed magnificently on two stories with a central atrium courtyard, typical of many colonial houses, allowing maximum air circulation. The sweep-ing Jackwood staircase and landings add a definitive grandeur to the interior, which sensitively blends modern-ized bathrooms with elegant Dutch antique furniture, fresh color with traditional architecture. The Kandy House ex-udes a sense of timelessness and stands as a celebration of the glorious possibilities when architecture embraces the past, present and the future.

from above to below, from left to right: outdoor living room,
garden, view into bedroom

from above to below, from left to right: bathroom with polished concrete finished, couryard seating area, bedroom, swimming pool

from above to below, from left to right: outdoor living area, interior with antique wood work, colonial house nestled in a coconut palm garden

bungalow-style house with veranda

Taru Villa

Bentota, Sri Lanka

Designer: Taru
Completion year: 2009
(refurbishment)
Materials: timber, glass

The observer's eye is fed with an exotic cornucopia of colors, with blue skies above, lush green gardens, a sparkling turquoise pool and numerous fascinating artifacts. Each villa is individually designed and decorated to generate a unique ambience and communal areas display carefully selected pieces of art and antiques that reflect and celebrate Sri Lanka's rich cultural heritage. The spaces are designed to be uncluttered and unpretentious to facilitate perfect relaxation. Numerous balconies and terraces overlook lily ponds and frangipani trees in the garden and offer views towards towering coconut palms and the ocean beyond.

from above to below, from left to right: swimming pool, contemporary living area, bedroom, staircase

from above to below, from left to right: exterior view from
swimming pool, veranda, bedroom with antique interiors

from above to below, from left to right: exterior corridor, main entrance, fragrant frangipani ("temple tree") garden, leading to swimming pool

ample veranda with view to swimming pool

Sun House

Galle, Sri Lanka

Designer: Taru
Completion year: 2009 (refurbishment)
Materials: wood, stone, concrete

Once the home of a Scottish spice merchant, this glorious house has been renovated to maintain its colonial charm and stylishness. Anyone entering the whitewashed walls of this intimate, bohemian oasis will be immediately endeared to its welcoming, laid-back elegance. Antique colonial furniture, four-poster beds and subtle, highly sophisticated décor lend an unforgettable charm to the

Sun House. Outdoors bathrooms and panoramic views towards distant hills, coconut jungle and the ocean invite the inhabitant to indulge in the property's superb elevated location. Two beautiful tropical gardens – a fragrant frangipani garden leading to the pool and a mango garden with a stunning view of Galle harbor – offer idyllic spaces in which to relax and sunbathe.

from above to below, from left to right: bathroom, interior with whitewashed walls, outdoor bathtub

from above to below: exterior view from driveway, interior
with antique colonial furniture

183

from above to below, from left to right: exterior view, view to planted garden from bed, exterior bedroom painted in cream

swimming pool surrounded by a lush green garden

Beach House

Tangalle, Sri Lanka

Architect: Douglas Johnson, in collaboration with Geoffrey Bawa
Completion year: 2009
Materials: wood, stone and concrete

The Beach House has direct access onto one of the finest beaches in the Indian Ocean, a large tropical garden and a stunning infinity pool. This idyllic villa lies among coconut palms on its own stretch of white beach near Tangalle on the south coast of Sri Lanka. The Beach House was once the tropical retreat of American artist Douglas Johnson, who lovingly restored the Dutch colonial bungalow with the help of Geoffrey Bawa, Sri Lanka's most renowned architect. Dark wooden colonial furniture is offset against a white colonnaded veranda and cushions in muted grays, blues and creams. Artistic details – shell mosaic mirrors, Johnson's collection of pictures and collages and quirky ornaments – help to make this house homely and inviting. A cozy piece of paradise by the sea.

from above to below, from left to right: oceanview from swimming pool, outdoor bathtub, bedroom features colonial artefacts and exquisite antiques, outdoor bathroom

interior with dark wooden colonial furniture

from above to below: interior view from lap pool, panoramic
oceanviews from deck

from above to below: loft-style living interior, floating wooden staircase

Villa of the Rising Sun

Koh Tao, Thailand

Architect: Saenz de Santamaria Designs
Completion year: 2011
Materials: wood (terraces), stone (floors), glass (wall panels) and concrete (floors)

This large and highly indulgent retreat, located on the tiny island of Koh Tao, Thailand, boasts a spacious open-plan living area with spectacular panoramic views of the open ocean and Koh Tao's sister island, Koh Nangyuan. The design couples loft-style living with a contemporary tropical ambience, incorporating multiple stylish bedrooms and bathrooms, expansive living areas, natural cooling and fan systems, and sun-lit terraces that entice sun-worshippers.

Nestled high amongst tropical vegetation, stone boulders and gardens of frangipanis, this sanctuary for the soul represents an inspired architectural endeavor that couples luxury with simplicity. The occupant is invited to seek a new harmony between humanity and nature, achieved only through total relaxation in these palm-shaded surroundings.

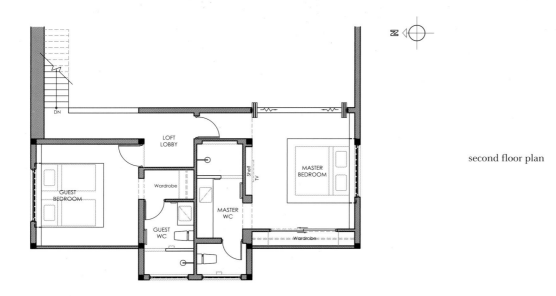

second floor plan

from above to below, from left to right: swimming pool covered with
a thatched roof, living/dining room with breathtaking view, bedroom,
bathroom featuring stone floors

from above to below: interior with pitched roof, interior/exterior boundaries blur between terrace and living room

from above to below: kitchen, bathroom, first floor plan

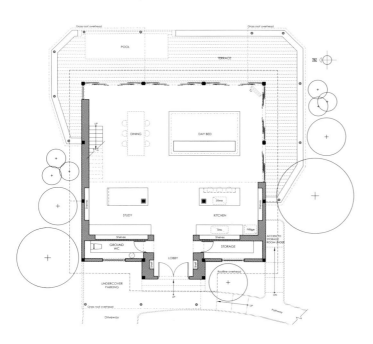

wooden pathway

aerial view of villas by night

Aleenta Phuket

Phuket, Thailand

Completion year: 2007
Materials: wood (terraces), glass (wall panels) and concrete (walls and floors)

Situated on a pristine and quiet beach, Aleenta Phuket-Phangnga is a set of luxury villas featuring stunning architecture and stylish interior design. Clean white façades mingle simply with dark wooden overhangs, terraces and roofs, and lush green vegetation. The stark white and brown of the architecture are complemented by the greens and blues of surrounding flora, sea and sky, a juxtaposition of colors that draws and astounds the eye of the onlooker. Each villa is located merely steps from the beach and offers a commanding sea view. Minimalist interior design rubs shoulders with Asian spirituality to create a relaxed and elegant environment. These villas represent the ultimate architectural achievement in combining aesthetics, luxury and comfort.

from above to below: bedroom with glass doors opening to boundary garden, night view from swimming pool to villa

from above to below, from left to right: bedroom with deck and oceanviews, living room with double-height ceiling, bathroom

from above to below, from left to right: villa with deck and
plunge pool, bathroom, interior detail

from above to below, from left to right: glass door opens out to swimming pool, pathway leads to beach deck, covered terrace

from left to right: built-in concrete sofa with cushions, interior
and exterior is blurred with glass sliding doors

view from swimming pool to deck and ocean

Villa of a Million Stars

Koh Tao, Thailand

Architect: Saenz de Santamaria Designs
Completion year: 2011
Materials: wood (terraces), stone (floors), glass (wall panels) and concrete (floors)

With a name to inspire the most wonderful of dreams, the Villa of a Million Stars is a trendy refuge in which to relax, tune in and turn off. Perched on a hillside on the tiny island of Koh Tao, Thailand, it offers spectacular views of Sairee town and the rolling waves of the open ocean. This stunning view is matched by the equally stunning designer interiors. Stylish bedrooms and bathrooms, a private swim-

ming pool, vast open-plan kitchen, dining and living areas, and dappled terraces await the world-weary traveler, who finds peace and tranquility in these elegant surroundings. Surrounded by tropical vegetation, frangipani gardens and natural boulders, the villa is seamlessly integrated into its landscape and offers the possibility of a new kind of relationship between man and the natural world.

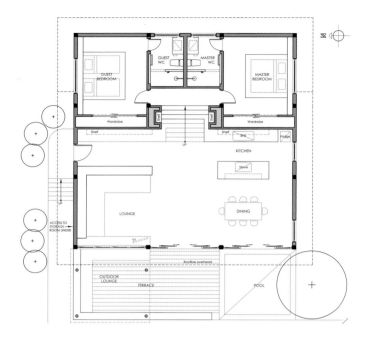

from above to below:
ground floor plan, open-plan interior

from above to below: outdoor living area, dining room with
ocean view

from above to below: exterior view, bedroom

from above to below, from left to right: pool detail, bathroom, concrete staircase

interior/exterior living areas

ocean view from pool

Sri Panwa

Phuket, Thailand

Architect: Habita Architects
Completion year: 2011
Materials: wood (terraces), stone (floors), glass (wall panels) and concrete (floors)

Sri Panwa enjoys an idyllic setting within 40 acres of lush tropical rainforest, perched high atop Cape Panwa. With each private pool villa carefully designed to showcase the true beauty of its coastal environment, these secluded residences have been hailed as one of Thailand's greatest venues, commanding breathtaking views of the surrounding Phuket islands and Andaman Sea. All the luxurious pool villas offer panoramic ocean views, while some boast full and uninterrupted 360-degree views of the sea. Interiors are designed to be simple and earthy, tropical and contemporary, while providing modern luxury living. Each structure is custom-built to follow the Cape's natural contours and is accompanied by an infinity pool. Every part of these villas has been designed and crafted to the highest standard, resulting in a series of architectural masterpieces in which living is pure pleasure.

from above to below, from left to right: infinity pool, outdoor shower, courtyard, wooden bridge leading to villas

from above to below: bathroom with glass sliding doors,
bedroom inside glass "box"

from above to below: interior and large decked terrace with pool, loft-like interior

from above to below: polished concrete kitchen counter, terrace with thatched roof

Villa of the Full Moon

Koh Tao, Thailand

Architect: Saenz de Santamaria Designs
Completion year: 2011
Materials: wood (terraces), stone (floors), glass (wall panels) and concrete (floors)

Commanding views over the ocean and a nearby island, the Villa of the Full Moon is a manifestation of decadent tropical grandeur. Surrounded by a garden of frangipanis, this stylish hideaway boasts a large decked terrace, an open-plan living area, a private swimming pool and two luxurious bedrooms with en-suite bathrooms. Set atop a hillside on the small Thai island of Koh Tao, it visually pro-

claims its uniqueness as an architectural structure, while blending into the stunning tropical landscape. Natural ventilation systems seek to cool the interior without the need for extensive and energy-consuming air conditioning. Thus, grandeur is tempered by environmental sensitivity, and architectural magnificence by a celebration of nature.

from above to below, from left to right: house blends into the
tropical landscape, breathtaking views, beds elevated on concrete
platform

from above to below: open-plan interior, ground floor plan

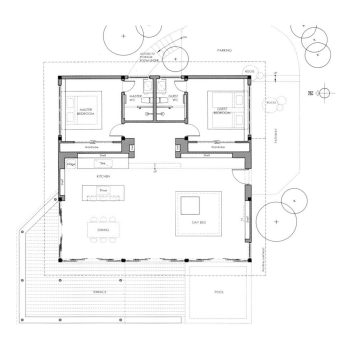

from above to below, from left to right: terrrace overlooking ocean, bird's eye view of swimming pool, spaces step down from the terrain

view from swimming pool to granite cobbled terrace walls

Villa Mayavee

Phuket, Thailand

Architect: Tierra Design
Structural engineer: Warnes Associate
M&E Engineer: Ove Arup (Thailand) Ltd
Lighting design: DJCoaliton
Completion year: 2009
Materials: granite cobbled walls, concrete, glass, wood

Located within the dramatic, undulating terrain of Phuket, far removed from the tourist areas, Villa Mayavee represents the ultimate tranquil living experience. While commanding panoramic views of the Andaman Sea and surrounding hills, the site also belongs to a lush tropical landscape sensitively established by the owner. Unique spatial experiences are generated by the Z-shaped structure at the center of the site, while cobbled walls meander through it. Inspired by traditional Thai architecture, the villa consists of separate pavilions but boasts an overall cohesion. The union of tradition and modernity is also manifest in the combination of stone and glass as primary materials. Indeed, this dwelling is a masterpiece of synthesis — past and present, seclusion and openness, manmade and natural co-exist in perfect harmony.

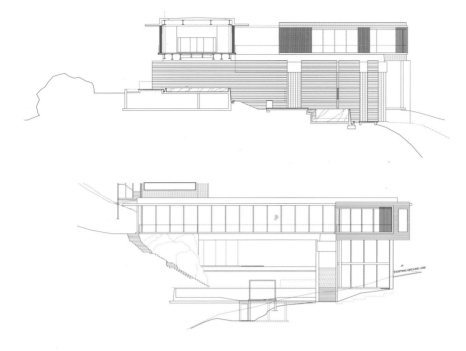

from above to below, from left to right: sections, entry reflection pond with a glass enclosed spiral staircase, bathroom with glass sliding doors, bedroom with breathtaking views

from left to right, from above to below: study room, master
bedroom seating area, living room appears to be floating by
the trees

from above to below: terrace pool overlooking tropical landscape,
living room

from above to below: terrace with thatched roof, kitchen

Villa of Green Palms

Koh Tao, Thailand

Architect: Saenz de Santamaria Designs
Completion year: 2011
Materials: wood (terraces), stone (floors), glass (wall panels) and concrete (floors)

A cozy retreat, the Villa of the Green Palms nestles amongst stone boulders and faces the broad expanse of the open ocean with views of Sairee town and the neighboring island of Koh Nangyuan. This intimate and unassuming villa offers the perfect setting for a romantic rendezvous. With its stylish interiors, expansive living spaces, private pool and wooden terraces, it represents the ultimate achievement in tropical architecture, both offering comfortable living and remaining sensitive to the natural environment. Rather than stridently proclaiming its own magnificence, this space enables the occupant to achieve a state of perfect relaxation in comfortable, elegant, palm-shaded surroundings.

from above to below: view from terrace, bedroom

from above to below: interior with concrete floors, pitched ceiling with exposed wooden structure, ground floor plan

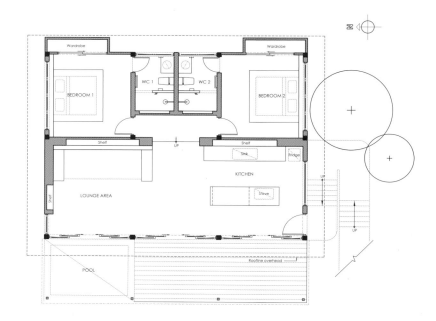

Architects'/Designers' Index

Bark Design Architects
>> 90

Studio 185 Sunrise Road
Tinbeerwah Queensland 4563
(Australia)
T +61.754710340
F +61.754710343
info@barkdesign.com.au
www.barkdesign.com.au

Geoffrey Bawa
>> 184

11, 33rd Lane, Off Bagatelle Road
Colombo 03 (Sri Lanka)
T +94.112589212
www.geoffreybawa.com

BGD Architects
>>96

Level 3 16 Queensland Avenue
Broadbeach Queensland 4218
(Australia)
T +61.755926188
F +61.755926133
bgd@bgdarchitects.com
www.bgdarchitects.com

Bernardes + Jacobsen Arquitetura
>> 54, 70

Rua Corcovado, 250
Jardim Botânico, Rio de Janeiro RJ
22460-050 (Brazil)
T +55.2125127743
bjrj@bja.com.br
www.bjaweb.com.br

Camarim Architects
>> 38

Rua da Madalena 80
1100-322 Lisbon (Portugal)
T +351.218825501
mail@camarim.pt
www.camarim.pt

Arthur Casas Studio
>> 44

Rua Itápolis 818
São Paulo, SP 01245-000 (Brazil)
T +55.1121827500
F +55.1136836540
sp@arthurcasas.com
www.arthurcasas.com

João Diniz Arquitetura
>> 48

Av. Pasteur, 89 Sl 809
- Sta Efigênia
Belo Horizonte, Minas Gerais
(Brazil)
jodin@accesso.com.br
www.joaodiniz.com.br

Juan Carlos Doblado
>> 74

Calle Miguel Dasso 139
Of. 702 Lima 27 (Peru)
doblado@juancarlosdoblado.com
www.juancarlosdoblado.com

**Roberto Fernandez and
Daniel Peyer**
>> 32

Gabriel Grinspum + Mariana Simas
>> 60

Alameda Tiête
505 – Cerqueira César
São Paulo, SP 01417-020 (Brazil)
T +55.1130813522
info@marciokogan.com.br
www.marciokogan.com.br

Guz Architects
>> 134, 156

3 Jalan Kelabu Asap
Singapore 278199 (Singapore)
T +65.64766110
F +65.74761229
guz@guzarchitects.com
www.guzarchitects.com

Habita Architects
>> 206

408/16 Rama 5 Road
Dusit, Bangkok 10300 (Thailand)
T +66.26686934
F +66.22437363
contact@habitaarchitects.com
www.habitaarchitects.com

K2LD Architects
>> 128, 144

261 Waterloo Street 02-32
Singapore 180261 (Singapore)
T +65.67387277
F +65.67387677
info@k2ld.com
www.k2ld.com

Khosla Associates
>> 106

No. 18 17th Main HAL 2nd A Stage
Indiranagar, Bangalore 560 008
(India)
T +91.8051161445
F +91.8025294951
info@khoslaassociates.com
www.khoslaassociates.com

MICD Associates/ Channa Daswatte
>> 172

56/1Rev. Dharmarathana, Mawatha
Madiwela – Kotte (Sri Lanka)
T +94.114406399
F +94.114308311
micd.assoicates@gmail.com
www.micda.com

Omiros One Architecture
>> 102

Ground Floor,
639 Little Bourke Street
Melbourne, VC 3000 (Australia)
T +61.396708899
F +61.396700808
info@omiros.com.au
www.o1a.com.au

OMM Design Workshop/ Andrew Makin and Janina Masojada
>> 86

Morningside, Durban (South Africa)
T +27.313035191

ONG&ONG Architects
>> 162

510 Thomson Road
SLF Building #11-00
Singapore 298135 (Singapore)
T +65.62588666
F +65.62598648
info@ong-ong.com
www.ong-ong.com

Andres Remy Arquitectos
>> 78, 82

T +54.1153850310
F +54.1147040411
info@andresremy.com
www.andresremy.com

Robles Arquitectos
>> 20

11270-1000 San José (Costa Rica)
T +506.22802255
F +506.22255418
info@roblesarq.com
www.roblesarq.com

Saenz de Santamaria Designs
>> 188, 200, 210, 218

P.O Box 70
Koh Tao, Surat Thani 84360
(Thailand)
T +66.856556523
stay@kohtaocasas.com
www.kohtaocasas.com

SCDA Architects
>> 116

8 Teck Lim Road
Singapore 088383 (Singapore)
scda@scdaarchitects.com
www.scdaarchitects.com

SPG Architects
>> 26

127 West 26th Street, #800
New York, NY10001 (USA)
T +1.212.3665500
F +1.212.3666559
contact@spgarchitects.com
www.spgarchitects.com

studio mk27 – Marcio Kogan + Suzana Glogowski + Samanta Cafardo
>> 64

Alameda Tiête
505 – Cerqueira César
São Paulo, SP 01417-020 (Brazil)
T +55.1130813522
info@marciokogan.com.br
www.marciokogan.com.br

Studio Mumbai Architects
>> 112

561/63 N.M.Joshi Marg
Byculla West, Mumbai 400011
(India)
T +91.2265777560
f +91.2223021973
contact@studiomumbai.com
www.studiomumbai.com

Taru
>> 176, 180

Tierra Design
>> 214

Unit 16B, 16th Floor, Piyaplace
Building
29/1 Soi Langsuan, Lumpini
Patumwan Bangkok 10330
(Thailand)
T +66.26585900
F +66.26585899
bangkok@tierradesign.com
www.tierradesign.com

Wallflower Architecture + Design
>> 138, 150

7500A Beach Road 15-303
The Plaza Singapore 19959
(Singapore)
T +65.62976883
F +65.62976332
wallflower@pacific.net.sg
www.wallflower.com.sg

WOHA
>> 122

29 Hongkong Street
Singapore 059668 (Singapore)
T +65.64234555
F +65.64234666
admin@woha.net
www.woha-architects.com

Wolfgang Ludes Architecture + Johannes Zingerle
>> 8

331 West 57th Street #353
New York, New York 10019 (USA)
T +1.212.9257584
studio@wolfgangludes.com
www.wolfgangludesarchitecture.com

Picture Credits

4 season info media	214–217
Binet, Hélène	112–115
Bingham Hall, Patrick	134–137, 156–161
Finotti, Leonardo	8–13, 14–19, 44–47, 48–53, 54–59, 70–73
Jackson, Gavin	168–171, 172–175, 176–179, 180–183, 184–187
Jansen, Remco	96–101
Courtesy of JMC Group	102–105
Jones, Christopher Frederick	90–95
Courtesy of K2LD Architects	128–133, 144–149
Kon, Nelson	64–69
Krobtong, Ekapon, Courtesy of Saenz de Santamaria Designs	188–193, 200–205, 210–213, 218–221
Kunz, Martin Nicholas	32–37, 86–89, 116–121, 122–127, 194–199, 206–209
Lim, Albert	138–143
Lindsay, Charles	26–31
Olshiati, Nic	38–43
Peral, Alejandro	82–85
Pucci, Sergio	20–25
Ramamrutham, Bharath Courtesy of Khosla Associates	106–111
Ramirez, Elsa	74–77
Courtesy of Andres Remy Arquitectos	78–81
Swalwell, Derek	162–167
Vannuchi, Pedro	60–65
Courtesy of Wallflower Architecture + Design	150–155

Cover: Christopher Frederick Jones
Backcover: from above to below, from left to right:
Martin Nicholas Kunz (a., b.l.), Patrick Bingham Hall

All other pictures were made available by the architects or designers.